D1552217

MONSTERS!

FRANKENSTEIN

BY FRANCES NAGLE

Gareth Stevens
PUBLISHING

Please visit our website, www.garethstevens.com. For a free color catalog of all our high-quality books, call toll free 1-800-542-2595 or fax 1-877-542-2596.

Cataloging-in-Publication Data

Names: Nagle, Frances.
Title: Frankenstein / Frances Nagle.
Description: New York : Gareth Stevens Publishing, 2016. | Series: Monsters! | Includes index.
Identifiers: ISBN 9781482448597 (pbk.) | ISBN 9781482448610 (library bound) | ISBN 9781482448603 (6 pack)
Subjects: LCSH: Shelley, Mary Wollstonecraft,--1797-1851.--Frankenstein--Juvenile literature. | Frankenstein films--History and criticism--Juvenile literature. | Frankenstein, Victor (Fictitious character)--Juvenile literature.
Classification: LCC PR5397.F73 N335 2016 | DDC 791.43'651--dc23

First Edition

Published in 2017 by
Gareth Stevens Publishing
111 East 14th Street, Suite 349
New York, NY 10003

Copyright © 2017 Gareth Stevens Publishing

Designer: Samantha DeMartin
Editor: Kristen Nelson

Photo credits: Cover, pp. 1, 15 Jeff Cameron Collingwood/Shutterstock.com; pp. 5, 9 Bob Orsillo/Shutterstock.com; p. 6 Hulton Archive/Hulton Archive/Getty Images; p. 7 Cecil/ Wikimedia Commons; pp. 11, 25 Universal Pictures/Moviepix/Getty Images; p. 13 John Kobal Foundation/Moviepix/Getty Images; p. 17 Silver Screen Collection/Moviepix/Getty Images; p. 19 Movie Poster Image Art/Moviepix/Getty Images; p. 21 (poster) Universal Pictures/ Wikimedia Commons; p. 21 (Karloff) Universal Studios/Wikimedia Commons; p. 23 Garry Gay/Photographer's Choice/Getty Images; p. 24 Universal History Archive/Universal Images Group/Getty Images; p. 27 20th Century Fox/Moviepix/Getty Images; p. 29 CBS Television Network/Wikimedia Commons; p. 30 carrie-nelson/Shutterstock.com.

Printed in the United States of America

CPSIA compliance information: Batch #CS16GS: For further information contact Gareth Stevens, New York, New York at 1-800-542-2595.

CONTENTS

IT'S ALIVE!

The scariest monster stories are the ones that seem like they could be true. Do you think a scientist might be able to make something living out of something dead? If you do, *Frankenstein* might be the scariest tale you'll find!

BEYOND THE MYTH

Don't get too scared. *Frankenstein* is fiction, which means it's a story about something that isn't true.

5

THE WRONG MONSTER

When most people say "Frankenstein," they mean a big, green monster that might be **dangerous**. But Frankenstein isn't a monster! Victor Frankenstein, a science student, is the main character in the book *Frankenstein* by Mary Wollstonecraft Shelley.

MARY SHELLEY

BEYOND THE MYTH

The **creature** commonly just called "Frankenstein"
should be called "Frankenstein's monster."

T. Holst, del.   W. Chevalier, sculp.

FRANKENSTEIN.

"By the glimmer of the half-extinguished
light, I saw the dull, yellow eye of the
creature open; it breathed hard, and a
convulsive motion agitated its limbs.
*** I rushed out of the room."

Page 43

7

PUTTING THE PIECES TOGETHER

Frankenstein begins with a man, Walton, meeting Victor Frankenstein near the North Pole. Frankenstein, who's sick, tells Walton that he created a monster using pieces of dead bodies. He gave the creature life using **electricity**.

BEYOND THE MYTH

In the 19th century, scientists were studying ways to use electricity to help the human body. Mary Shelley knew about this before she wrote *Frankenstein*.

Frankenstein tells Walton the rest of the story: Upset by what he's done, Frankenstein ends up leaving the monster in his home. The monster gets out while he's gone. Soon after, Frankenstein hears his brother William has been killed. He sees the monster near where William died.

BEYOND THE MYTH

Frankenstein was published in 1818. In 1831, Mary Shelley claimed the story came to her late one night, all at once. Most people believe she made this up to make her story sound more exciting.

11

The monster follows
Frankenstein to where he's
traveling in the mountains.
The monster says he killed
William to get back at
Frankenstein for creating him.
The monster asks Frankenstein
to make him a **mate**.
Frankenstein does—but then
destroys her.

BEYOND THE MYTH

The book's full title is *Frankenstein; Or, The Modern Prometheus*. Prometheus was a figure from Greek **myths** who gave people fire.

13

KILLER ON THE LOOSE

The monster is angry and starts to ruin Frankenstein's life. First, he kills Frankenstein's friend, and Frankenstein is blamed. Then, the monster kills Frankenstein's new wife on their wedding night. Frankenstein promises to find and kill his creation.

BEYOND THE MYTH

Today, using body parts of those who've died is commonplace in hospitals all over the world. In fact, people who've been hurt very badly may be able to get a face **transplant**!

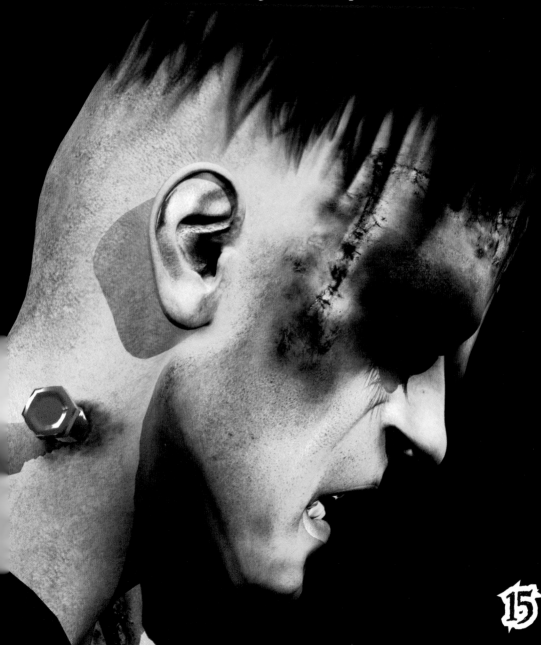

LONELY MONSTER

Frankenstein follows the monster north, gets sick, and meets Walton. When Frankenstein dies, Walton finds the monster crying over his creator's body. The monster says he feels bad about what happened. He's lonely. The monster goes even further north to die.

BEYOND THE MYTH

"Mad scientists" likely scare people because they're trying to learn something other people don't think they should know, such as how to bring the dead back to life.

17

THE BIG SCREEN

Frankenstein is one of the most popular stories used for scary movies! The first one was made in 1910. The inventor Thomas Edison produced it. It's less than 13 minutes long.

BEYOND THE MYTH

In Jewish stories, a golem is a creature made by magic to work for its creator. The early German movies *The Golem* and *Homunculus* deal with this idea and affected later *Frankenstein* movies.

THE GOLEM

19

In 1915, a silent movie called *Life Without a Soul* was the first full-length movie made of Mary Shelley's book. The most famous movie of *Frankenstein* came out in 1931. It starred Boris Karloff as the monster.

BEYOND THE MYTH

Earl Bakken saw the movie *Frankenstein* and loved the scientist character. He became a true-life Frankenstein, later inventing the wearable pacemaker, which uses electricity to control the heartbeat.

BORIS KARLOFF

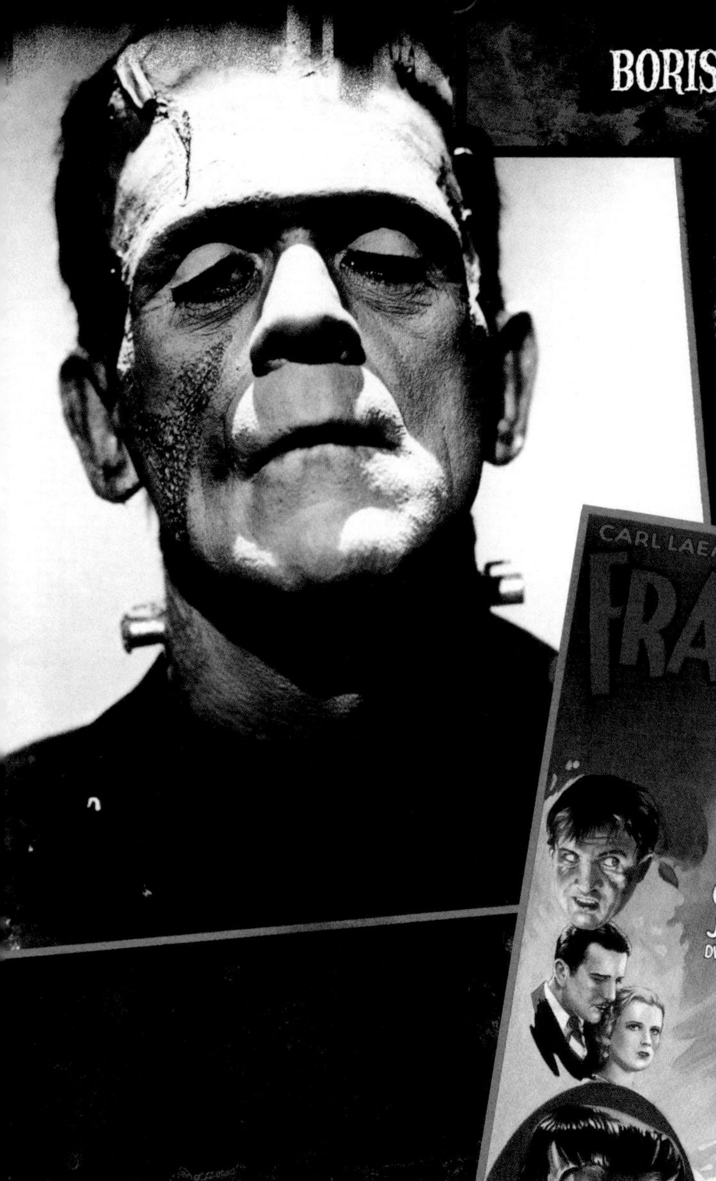

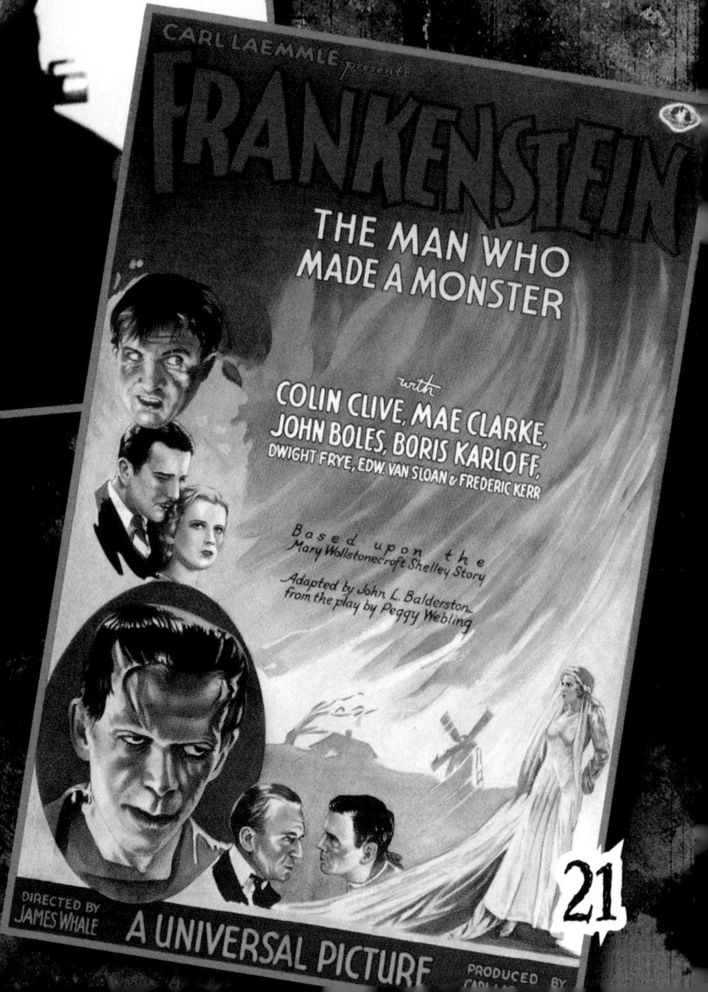

The Frankenstein Halloween costumes of today are based on Boris Karloff as Frankenstein's monster. He was very tall and wore all black. He had bolts in his neck, a flat-looking head, and a thick forehead.

BEYOND THE MYTH

In the movie *Frankenstein*, the monster is given the brain of a criminal, or a person who has broken the law. This explains in the movie why he does so much wrong.

In 1935, *The Bride of Frankenstein* hit the big screen. Boris Karloff starred in this movie as the monster, too. In it, the monster finally gets the mate he asked Frankenstein for!

BEYOND THE MYTH

Frankenstein's son finds his father's monster in the 1939 movie *Son of Frankenstein*. He brings it back to life with awful results!

FUNNY MONSTER?

Many believe *Young Frankenstein* to be one of the funniest movies ever. It starred Gene Wilder as Frankenstein's grandson. In 2007, a musical of the movie began its run on Broadway and was a huge hit!

BEYOND THE MYTH

Even though it came out in 1974 and could have been
in color, *Young Frankenstein* is in black and white.

The main character on the 1960s TV show *The Munsters* looked a lot like Frankenstein's monster, too. The family on the show was made up of monsters, however, so he didn't stand out too much!

BEYOND THE MYTH

In 2012, the movie *Frankenweenie* told the story of a little boy who brought his dog back to life. He used lightning!

THE MUNSTERS

29

Look Like
Frankenstein's Monster

HEAD SCAR

BLACK, FLAT HAIR

GREEN SKIN

BOLTS IN NECK

BLACK SUIT WITH
BIG SHOULDERS

FOR MORE INFORMATION

BOOKS

Jantner, Janos. *Drawing Monsters from Great Books.* New York, NY: PowerKids Press, 2013.

Sierra, Sergio A. *Frankenstein by Mary Shelley: A Dark Graphic Novel.* Berkeley Heights, NJ: Enslow Publishers, 2013.

Small, Cathleen. *Frankenstein's Monster.* New York, NY: Cavendish Square Publishing, 2016.

WEBSITES

The Legend of Frankenstein
kidzworld.com/article/24907-the-legend-of-frankenstein
Read more about the story of Frankenstein and his monster.

Mythological Monsters
monsters.monstrous.com
Use the links on this website to learn about many more monstrous creatures based on myths and stories from around the world.

GLOSSARY

creature: an animallike being

dangerous: unsafe

electricity: energy used to power many things, such as lights

mate: one of two creatures that come together to produce babies

myth: a tale or story

transplant: a medical operation in which a body part is taken from one person and given to another

INDEX